ASSASSINATION CLASSROOM

YUSEI MATSUI

1

TIME FOR ASSASSINATION

ASSASSINATION CLASSROOM 1 CONTENTS

(ANSWER SHEET)

Grade 3 Class E Name CONTENTS Score

Class 1 Killing Time in Homeroom

NOW!!
KLACK
KLACK
KLACK
EECH

CLASS 1 KILLING TIME IN HOMEROOM
KLACK
SCR

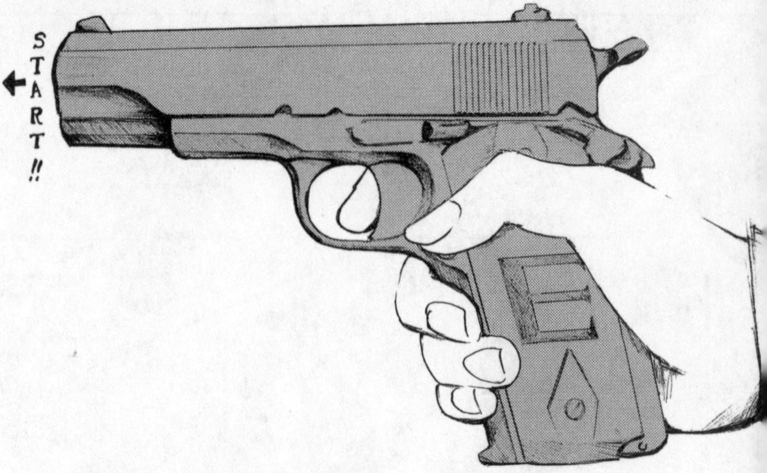
START!!

GET READY!!
KLCK
KLACK
GRIN
WE ARE...
...ASSAS-SINS.
gulp.
FI-I-I-RE!!!!
POW
POW
POW POW POW POW POW

POW
SO I GUESS WE'RE NOT DOING THE PLEDGE THEN...
POW POW
POW POW POW
POW
Attendance
POW
OKAY. YOU MAY KEEP SHOOTING WHILE I TAKE ATTENDANCE.
ISOGAI.
HUH?
POW POW POW
I'M SORRY, I CAN'T HEAR YOU OVER ALL THESE GUNSHOTS. COULD YOU SPEAK UP, PLEASE?
UM ...
HERE!!
POW POW POW POW
POW
OKANO.
HERE !!
KATA-OKA.
HERE !!

EVERYONE'S HERE... AND ON TIME!
WONDERFUL! I'M SO HAPPY!
ZLIP
HE'S TOO FAST!!
ALL THOSE BULLETS... AND WE MISSED?!
DINK
WE'RE ASSASSINS. AND OUR TARGET IS...
...OUR TEACHER.
DINK
DINK
YOU MISSED. AGAIN.
GRIN
THAT'S TOO BAD.
YOU'RE RELYING TOO MUCH ON THE "SPRAY AND PRAY" METHOD.
...
CONSIDER YOUR LINE OF SIGHT...
...WHERE YOU'RE AIMING...
...YOUR TRIGGER FINGER...
YOUR METHOD IS TOO PREDICTABLE.

YOU HAVE TO COME UP WITH A MORE ORIGINAL PLAN.
I'M TOO QUICK FOR YOU.
I CAN MOVE AT MACH 20, REMEMBER?
ARE YOU REALLY DODGING ALL THOSE BULLETS?
WELL, THEY'RE MORE LIKE BB'S THAN BULLETS...
MAYBE WE'RE HITTING YOU, BUT YOU'RE JUST PRETEND-ING WE DIDN'T!
YEAH! YOU'RE CHEATING!
BOO! BOO!
...
OKAY. SOMEONE PLEASE HAND ME A GUN THAT'S LOADED.
LIKE I SAID...
...THESE BULLETS—BB'S—ARE HARMLESS TO YOU...
KCHIK

BLAM
SPLORCH
BUT THEY WERE DESIGNED ESPECIALLY FOR ME.
SQUIGGL SQUIGGL SQUIGGL
THEY CAN CUT THROUGH ME LIKE PUDDING.
HEH.
OF COURSE, I CAN REGENERATE LOST LIMBS AND SUCH IN A FEW SECONDS.
ZLORP
BUT I WOULDN'T WANT ANYBODY TO ACCIDENTALLY SHOOT THEIR EYE OUT WITH THESE.
SO PLEASE DON'T USE THE GUN INSIDE THE CLASSROOM UNLESS YOU ARE TRYING TO KILL ME.

WOM
WOM
I HOPE YOU CAN KILL ME...
...BEFORE GRADUATION.
RING
RING
RING
RING
IT'S TIME TO START CLASS.
NOW PLEASE PUT AWAY YOUR GUNS, PICK UP ALL THE BULLETS, AND LET'S GET THIS ROOM IN ORDER.
KUNUGIGAOKA JUNIOR HIGH, CLASS 3-E IS THE ASSASSINATION CLASSROOM.
IT'S WEIRD, BUT WE'VE KINDA GOTTEN USED TO IT.

OKAY... KIMURA...
WHICH OF MY TENTACLES IS POINTING TO THE SENTENCE WITH THE RELATIVE CLAUSE?
Grammar
...
THE BLUE ONE?
CORRECT!!
THE "WHO" IN THIS SENTENCE BEGINS THE RELATIVE CLAUSE.
SO...HOW DID WE END UP IN THIS SITUATION?
HEY...
...NAGISA!
IT'S NOON...
...AND YOU CAN STILL SEE THE CRESCENT MOON.
TWO THINGS HAPPENED...
...AT THE START OF OUR THIRD YEAR.

THE MOON !!
WHAT HAPPENED TO THE MOON?!
SEVENTY PERCENT OF THE MOON IS JUST... GONE!! IT'LL NEVER BE FULL AGAIN!!
NICE TO MEET YOU.
I'M THE ONE WHO DISINTEGRATED PART OF THE MOON.
AND NEXT YEAR AT THIS TIME I'M GOING TO DO THE SAME THING TO YOUR PLANET EARTH.
ALSO, I'M YOUR NEW TEACHER. I HOPE WE GET ALONG WELL.

AS IF THAT WASN'T STRANGE ENOUGH...
...THEN IT GOT WEIRD!
MY NAME'S KARASUMA. I'M FROM THE MINISTRY OF DEFENSE.
WHAT I'M ABOUT TO TELL YOU...
...IS EXTREMELY CONFIDENTIAL. THIS IS A TOP SECRET OPERATION, AND I NEED YOUR HELP.
TO PUT IT BLUNTLY...
...I WANT YOU TO KILL THIS MONSTER!!

UM...
EXCUSE ME...
IS THIS GUY SOME KIND OF, UH, ALIEN WHO'S COME TO, LIKE, DESTROY THE PLANET?
HOW RUDE!
FSSST
I WAS BORN AND RAISED ON EARTH!
SORRY, THAT INFORMATION IS CLASSIFIED.
BUT HE'S TELLING YOU THE TRUTH.
ONLY THE WORLD LEADERS KNOW OF THIS.
SO WE'RE TRYING TO KILL HIM...
...BEFORE THE WORLD FINDS OUT, CAUSING A MASS PANIC.
ALSO, HE DESTROYED MOST OF THE MOON...
...AND HE PLANS TO DESTROY THE EARTH NEXT YEAR AFTER YOUR GRADUATION.
ZLIP
IN OTHER WORDS, YOUR ASSIGNMENT IS TO...

SWISH
...ASSAS-SINATE YOUR TEACHER.
SW
ISH
AS YOU CAN SEE...
...HE'S INCREDIBLY FAST!!
SWISH
PLUK
PLUK
SWISH
RIGHT NOW HE'S TRIMMING MY EYEBROWS WITH AMAZING ACCURACY AND SKILL!
SWISH
HE'S POWERFUL ENOUGH TO BLOW UP THE MOON...
...AND TO FLY AT MACH 20!!
IN OTHER WORDS...
...IF HE REALLY TRIED TO ESCAPE US...
...WE'D NEVER BE ABLE TO CATCH HIM—UNTIL IT WAS TOO LATE!

BUT THAT WOULD BE...
...BO-RING.
SNAP
SO I MADE A PROPOSAL TO THE WORLD LEADERS.
ALTHOUGH I HAVE NO INTENTION OF GETTING KILLED...
TAP TAP
...I WANT TO BE THE TEACHER OF CLASS 3-E AT KUNUGIGAOKA JUNIOR HIGH.
WHY?!
WE... DON'T KNOW.
BUT WE ACCEPTED HIS OFFER...
...UNDER THE CONDITION THAT HE NEVER HARM ANY STUDENTS.
AT LEAST WHILE HE'S TEACHING...
...WE'LL BE ABLE TO KEEP AN EYE ON HIM.

AND BEST OF ALL...
...THIRTY OF YOU...
...CAN ATTEMPT TO KILL HIM EVERY DAY AT CLOSE RANGE!!
BLAM
KRCK
NAKA-MURA...
FSSST
DIDN'T I TELL YOU THAT YOU MAY ONLY TRY TO KILL ME AS LONG AS IT DOESN'T INTERFERE WITH YOUR STUDIES?
GO STAND IN THE CORNER.
SOR-RY...
UGH. I HATE HOW RED HIS FACE GETS WHEN HE'S MAD.
IT WAS SURREAL.
WHY DID THIS THING WANT TO BE OUR TEACHER?
WHY DO WE HAVE TO ASSAS-SINATE HIM?!
AND WHAT'S IN IT FOR US?

TEN BILLION IN COLD CASH!!
IF YOU KILL HIM!
BELIEVE ME WHEN I SAY ASSASSINATING HIM WILL SAVE THE WORLD!
¥?!
Ten b-b-b...
LUCKILY FOR YOU, HE DOESN'T CONSIDER YOU CHILDREN A THREAT.
GRIN
LOOK.
SEE THOSE GREEN STRIPES? HE DOESN'T THINK YOU CAN DO IT.
NEAT! HE'S LIKE A CHAMEL-EON!
OF COURSE I DON'T.
YOU'RE NOT AN ARMY.
WHEN I WAS ATTACKED BY A STATE-OF-THE-ART FIGHTER PLANE...
SQUEEGEE SQUEEGEE
...I WAXED IT IN MIDAIR FOR THEM.
WHY DID YOU POLISH IT FOR THEM?!

JUST STRIKE WHILE HIS GUARD IS DOWN.
WE'LL GIVE YOU SPECIAL WEAPONRY—HARMLESS TO YOU, FATAL TO HIM!
EXACTLY.
BUT REMEMBER, THIS IS *TOP SECRET*. YOU MUST TELL *NO ONE!*
WE DON'T HAVE A LOT OF TIME.
AND NOWHERE TO GO IF HE DESTROYS THE EARTH.
SO UNTIL THEN...
...I WANT ALL OF YOU TO LIVE THE REMAINING YEAR OF YOUR LIFE AS PRODUCTIVELY AS POSSIBLE!
RING
RING
RING
RING

LUNCH-TIME.
I'M GOING TO ZIP OVER TO CHINA FOR SOME MAPO TOFU.
IF ANYONE WANTS TO TRY TO ASSASSINATE ME DURING OUR LUNCH BREAK, FEEL FREE TO GIVE ME A BUZZ ON MY CELL PHONE.
WIIIZZZ
ZOOOOOOF
MUST BE NICE TO BE ABLE TO FLY AT MACH 20...
AT THAT SPEED, IT'S ABOUT A TEN-MINUTE FLIGHT TO SICHUAN PROVINCE TO GET AUTHENTIC MAPO TOFU.
NO WONDER THEY CAN'T SHOOT HIM DOWN WITH A MISSILE.

SCRTCH SCRTCH
WHADDYA KNOW... THAT CRAZY FREAK IS GRADING OUR TESTS WHILE FLYING.
SERI-OUSLY?!
YEAH.
HE LIKED MY ANSWER. HE EVEN DREW A LITTLE OCTOPUS NEXT TO IT.
Perfect!
YOU KNOW, HE'S NOT A BAD TEACHER...
YEAH.
I TRIED TO ASSASSIN-ATE HIM AFTER SCHOOL BUT HE STARTED TUTOR-ING ME IN MATH...
AND I ACED THE TEST!
WELL...
YEAH...
BUT WE'RE STILL CLASS E.
SO WHY WORK SO HARD FOR NOTHING?
EXACTLY.
NEW HOLLOW ENGLISH

WE HAVE TO ASSAS-SINATE...
...SOME WEIRD SUPER-OCTOPUS THING...
Chemistry
...THAT FOR SOME REASON IS OUR TEACHER.
WELL...
...THE STUDENTS OF CLASS E...
...ARE A LITTLE DIFFERENT ACTUALLY...
KIND OF LIKE US...
WE MAY BE PART-TIME ASSASSINS, BUT WE'RE STILL FULL-TIME STUDENTS.
HEY, NAGISA...
TNK

C'MERE.
LET'S GO OVER THE PLAN.
...
OKAY.
YOU DO YOUR HOMEWORK LIKE I ASKED?
YOU FIGURE OUT WHAT IT MEANS WHEN HIS FACE CHANGES COLOR?
SORT OF...
WE ALREADY KNOW WHEN HIS FACE HAS GREEN STRIPES, HE'S NOT TAKING US SERI-OUSLY.

WHEN A STUDENT MAKES A MISTAKE, HIS FACE TURNS DARK PURPLE.
AND BRIGHT RED WHEN A STUDENT GETS THE RIGHT ANSWER.
THE INTER-ESTING COLOR IS AFTER LUNCH. THAT'S WHEN IT TURNS—
I DON'T NEED TO KNOW—*YOU* DO.
MY PLAN IS SIMPLE.
YOU STAB HIM...
...WHEN HIS GUARD IS DOWN.
ME...?
B-BUT... B...
OH, COME ON...
GLARE
WE'RE CLASS E, REMEMBER?

THE SCHOOL'S LOSERS AND REJECTS.
THE "END CLASS."
旧校舎
STUCK IN SOME OLD CLASSROOM YOU HAVE TO CLIMB A MOUNTAIN TO GET TO.
...AND TREATED LIKE CRAP BY EVERYONE—INCLUDING THE TEACHERS!
EVEN IF WE ALL STARTED WORKING RIGHT NOW AND POOLED OUR PAYCHECKS ...
YANK
...WE'D NEVER SEE 10 BILLION BUCKS IN OUR LIFETIME!
WE ARE GETTIN'...
ZLIP
...OUT OF THIS DUMP ANY WAY WE CAN!

ANY WAY...
...WE CAN.
DON'T LET ME DOWN, NAGISA!
...
HA HAHA HAHA ...
NAGISA'S BEING SENT TO CLASS E.
TIME TO UNFRIEND HIM...
旧校舎 1km
本校舎
Class Transfer Notice
Shiota Nagisa
Because your academic achievement does not meet the standards of this school, you are hereby transferred
WHOA.
HE'S DONE FOR.
I DON'T WANT OTHER PEOPLE TO THINK I KNOW HIM.

ZWOOP
WHOA !!
WEL-COME BACK...
WHAT'S WITH THE MISSILE ?
A SOU-VENIR.
THE NAVY WAS WAITING FOR ME IN THE SEA OF JAPAN.
WOW ...
IT MUST BE TOUGH BEING EVERY-ONE'S TARGET.
NAH.
TINK
I LOOK AT IT THIS WAY...
...BEING EVERYONE'S TARGET PROVES HOW POWERFUL I AM.
!

NOW THEN...
IT'S TIME FOR FIFTH PERIOD.
UM...
YEAH...
HE...
...DOESN'T UNDERSTAND.
AT LEAST...
...PEOPLE RECOGNIZE HIS POWER.
HE DOESN'T GET WHAT IT'S LIKE...
LUB DUB
...TO BE HUMAN...
...AND IGNORED BY EVERYONE.

YOU DESTROYED MY REPUTATION, YOU KNOW.
LUB DUB
AT LEAST NOW...
LUB DUB
...I WON'T HAVE TO SEE YOU ANYMORE.
LUB DUB
LUB
DUB
TING
I MIGHT ACTUALLY BE ABLE TO KILL HIM.
TING
TING
AFTER ALL...
...HE'LL IGNORE ME TOO—UNTIL IT'S TOO LATE.

Assention/Past
Auxiliary Verb
Were
LET'S WRITE SOME FREE-VERSE POETRY.
I'D LIKE YOU TO END ALL YOUR POEMS WITH THE WORD "TENTACLES."
PLEASE BRING THEM TO ME WHEN YOU'RE DONE.
I'LL BE CHECKING GRAMMAR AS WELL AS YOUR USE OF METAPHORS AND SIMILES.
The flower petals fell like colored snow. The vines writhed up from the ground like tentacles.
IF YOU'RE DONE, YOU MAY LEAVE FOR THE DAY.
"N-T... There's a big difference."
Oh, I get that reference!

I HAVE A QUESTION.
HM ...?
WHAT IS IT, KAYANO?
I KNOW THE SCHOOL YEAR HAS ALREADY STARTED, BUT...
WE CAN'T REALLY CALL OUR TEACHER "STRANGE OCTOPUS-THING WE HAVE TO KILL."
...WHAT'S YOUR NAME?
THAT'S A BIT LONG, YES...
YOU KNOW... I DON'T HAVE A NAME!
WHY DON'T YOU THINK OF ONE FOR ME?
BUT AFTER YOU FINISH YOUR POEM.
OKAY.
PSSSSF

KLTTR
AH.
DONE ALREADY, NAGISA?
GRIN
FWIP
THERE'S A TIME WHEN HIS FACE TURNS LIGHT PINK...
FWIP
...IT'S AFTER LUNCH, WHEN WE ALL FEEL A LITTLE SLEEPY.
FWIP
EVERY-BODY'S MORE RELAXED... HIM TOO.
Ah
THIS IS PROBABLY THE TIME OF DAY HE LOWERS HIS GUARD THE MOST.

LUB DUB
NA-GISA...
THE STUDENTS IN CLASS E ARE THE LOSERS... THE OUTCASTS...
HE'S GOING TO DO IT!!
LUB DUB
WE HAVE TO SHOW THEM THEY'RE WRONG.
LUB DUB
WE HAVE TO PROVE TO EVERYONE THAT "WE CAN DO IT IF WE REALLY TRY."
LUB DUB
I'D KILL FOR THAT CHANCE!

SWISH
STAB
I HAVE TO GET THEM TO NOTICE ME...
I TOLD YOU AL-READY...
YOU NEED TO COME UP WITH A BETTER...

...NO MATTER WHAT!
HUG
...PLAN.
YOIKS!
KLNCH
A BB GRENADE!!
THE ASSAS-SINATION SPECIAL!!
GOTCHA!!

BOOM

YEAH! WE DID IT!
ZIP
THAT 10 BILLION IS MINE!!
SUCKS TO BE YOU!!
I BET HE WASN'T EXPECTING THAT!!
HEY, TERASAKA! WHAT DID YOU GIVE NAGISA?
HUH?
A TOY GRENADE...
...STUFFED WITH GUNPOWDER...
...AND THOSE SPECIAL BB'S. MADE QUITE A MESS.
WHAT...?!
DON'T WORRY, IT'S JUST A LITTLE EXPLOSION...
I'LL COVER NAGISA'S MEDICAL BILLS WITH MY 10 BILLION.

WHAT THE...?
NOT A SCRATCH OR BURN OR ANY-THING...
Uhn...
AND WHAT IS THIS FILMY STUFF COVERING NAGISA?
IT LOOKS LIKE IT'S PART OF THE OCTOPUS, BUT...
RIP
RMBL
RMBL
RMBL
RMBL
RMBL
RMBL
ACTUALLY, I SHED MY SKIN ONCE A MONTH OR SO.
I COVERED THE BOMB WITH IT TO ABSORB THE EXPLOSION.
I DON'T LIKE HAVING TO DO THAT.

AND THEN WE SAW A NEW COLOR...
KRCKL
KRCKL
...ON HIS FACE...
KRCKL
...PITCH BLACK!
KRCKL
HE WAS FURIOUS.
KRCKL
TERASAKA! YOSHIDA! MURAMATSU!
YOU CAME UP WITH THIS PLAN, DIDN'T YOU?!
WHAT?
N-NO ...!
IT WAS NAGISA!

WHOOSH
WFF
WFF
WFF

WFF

SHOOP

TERASAKA
TNK
YOSHIDA
TNK
MURAMATSU
TNK
HEY ...
WHAT ...?
YOSHIDA
MURAMATS
TERASAKA
THE NAME PLATES... OFF OUR HOUSES?!
BUT IF YOU TRY TO ASSASSINATE ME LIKE THAT AGAIN...
I MADE A DEAL...
I PROMISED I WOULD NEVER HARM ANY OF *YOU*...
MAEHA
NAKAMURA
...LET ME REMIND YOU THAT *EVERYONE ELSE* IS FAIR GAME!
HAYAMI
KLTTR
KLTTR KLTTR
KURAHASHI
KIMURA
SUGINO

GRIN
YOUR FAMILY... YOUR FRIENDS...
MAYBE THE WHOLE WORLD... EXCEPT YOU.
WE ONLY NEEDED FIVE SECONDS TO REALIZE...
...THERE WAS NO ESCAPE FOR US, NO MATTER WHERE WE WENT.
AND THE ONLY WAY TO KEEP EVERYONE SAFE...
...WAS TO KILL HIM!!

WH...
WHAT ARE YOU?!
YOU'RE A NASTY CREA-TURE!
YOU DIS-INTEGRATE MOST OF THE MOON AND TELL US YOU'RE GOING TO BLOW UP THE EARTH...
WHY SHOULDN'T WE USE NASTY METHODS TO KILL A NASTY CREATURE?!
NASTY?
I THOUGHT YOUR IDEA WAS WONDERFUL. BRILLIANT.
STRTCH

I GIVE YOU TEN OUT OF TEN FOR YOUR SMOOTH AND NATURAL MOVEMENTS UP UNTIL YOU GRABBED ME.
I WAS TOTALLY CAUGHT OFF-GUARD.
PAT PAT
ESPECIALLY YOUR CONTRIBUTION, NAGISA.
UH-HUH...
HOWEVER ...!
KRCKL
THE REST OF YOU DIDN'T EVEN CONSIDER NAGISA'S SAFETY...
AND NAGISA LET YOU TAKE ADVANTAGE OF HIM!
YOU'RE BETTER THAN THAT...ALL OF YOU!
URK.

I WANT YOU TO ASSASSINATE ME WITH A METHOD THAT BRINGS A SMILE TO YOUR FACE, ONE THAT YOU CAN TAKE PRIDE IN.
YOU'RE MORE THAN CAPABLE OF THAT.
JUST TAKE A FEW WORDS OF ADVICE FROM YOUR TARGET...

HE SCOLDED US AT MACH 20...
...AND PRAISED US.
THIS CRAZY TENTACLED TEACHER...
...THIS WEIRD TEACHER...
...WAS ACTUALLY TAKING A LONG HARD LOOK AT US...
SIZZ

IF YOU'RE WILLING TO GIVE ME YOUR TIME...
...I'D LIKE YOU TO... TEACH THE CHILDREN FOR ME...
...
WHAT WONDERFUL TENTACLES YOU HAVE!!
WITH THESE ...
I'M SURE YOU'LL BECOME ...
...A FINE ...
... TEACHER...
FSSS

WELL THEN... I HAVE A QUESTION FOR YOU, NAGISA...
I HAVE NO INTENTION OF GETTING KILLED.
I'LL ENJOY TEACHING YOU UNTIL THE END OF THE SCHOOL YEAR, AND THEN I'LL DESTROY THE WORLD.
SO WHAT DO YOU NEED TO DO TO PREVENT THAT FROM HAPPENING?
I NEVER THOUGHT OF MYSELF AS AN ASSASSIN BEFORE...
...AND THERE ARE A LOT OF THINGS I HAVE TO LEARN TO BECOME A PROPER ONE...
KLNCH
BUT SOME-HOW I KNOW...

I'LL...
...KILL YOU BEFORE I LET THAT HAPPEN!
...THAT THIS TEACHER...
...WILL BE HAPPY TO SEE ME TRY.
THEN LET'S SEE YOU KILL ME RIGHT NOW.
I'LL LET YOU GO HOME EARLY IF YOU DO!!
WE ARE ASSAS-SINS.
Phew.
AND OUR TARGET IS OUR TEACHER.

A TEACHER WHO CAN'T BE KILLED...
"SENSEI" MEANS "TEACHER"...
"KORO-SENAI" MEANS "CAN'T BE KILLED."
HOW ABOUT IF WE CALL YOU...
..."KORO SENSEI"? IT'S A PUN!
KORO SENSEI AND THE ASSASSINATION CLASSROOM.
IF WE ATTACK HIM NOW, HE'LL POLISH OFF OUR FAMILIES LIKE OUR NAME-PLATES.
I CAN'T GO HOME...
AND THE SCHOOL BELL WILL TOLL AGAIN TOMORROW.

Koro Sensei

- Date of Birth: Unknown
- Height: Around 10 feet if he stretches
- Weight: Lighter than he looks
- Career History: Agent of destruction/ Teacher of Class E
- Hobby/Skill: Supersonic speed cruising
- Motto: Education and Assassination in One!
- Weakness: Unknown
- Strong Point: Easy to draw

Class 2 No Time to Strike Out

Top Secret Assassination Orders

This criminal element destroyed our moon.
And vows to destroy the earth in a year's time.
Beware of his numerous extraordinary abilities.
ten billion dollar award for him, dead not alive.

THE AMERICAN NEWSPAPERS ARE FULL OF ARTICLES ABOUT THE MOON'S DESTRUCTION AS WELL...
SLUURP
The K.Y. Times
Moon Havoc Continues...
I WISH THEY'D PUT SOMETHING MORE INTERESTING ON THEIR FRONT PAGE.
EVERY MORNING BEFORE HOMEROOM, HE KICKS BACK AND RELAXES BEHIND THE SCHOOL BUILDING...
...WITH AN AMERICAN NEWSPAPER AND A FRESH DRINK HE PICKED UP IN HAWAII AT MACH 20.
IT'S JUST LIKE YOU TOLD ME.
THANKS, NAGISA.
SURE.
GOOD LUCK, SUGINO!
OH YEAH!
THAT COOL 10 BILLION IS MINE!!
GRIP

WE ARE...
STRTCH
...ASSAS-SINS.
AND OUR TARGET IS...
WHO
OOSH
...OUR TEACHER.

GOOD MORNING...
...NAGISA, SUGINO...
COME NOW...
YOU SHOULD ALWAYS REPLY WHEN SOMEONE GREETS YOU.
...
RSSTL
GOOD MORNING, KORO SENSEI!
HUH?!
WHA—?!
I LIKE YOUR IDEA OF COVERING THE BALL IN ANTI-"ME" BB'S.
BUT UNLIKE AN AIR GUN, IT DOESN'T MAKE A SOUND WHEN THROWN.
FSSSSS

Slow Motion Replay
BUT...
I HAD SOME TIME BEFORE THE BALL REACHED ME...
FWA
ZZIP
AND SINCE I CAN'T TOUCH THOSE BB'S WITHOUT HURTING MYSELF...
KREEK
THNK
ZOOSH
Courage
KREEK
Courage
Courage
RSTL RSTL

I WENT OVER...
...TO THE STOREROOM TO GET A BASEBALL GLOVE.
WHAT THE ...?!
I REALLY DO HOPE YOU MANAGE TO KILL ME...
...BEFORE GRADUATION.
TIME FOR HOMEROOM.
OKAY.
SURE ...

OUR MISSION...
...IS TO KILL OUR TEACHER.
IF WE SUCCEED, WE GET 10 BILLION DOLLARS!
HEY, NAGISA!
I HEARD SUGINO BLEW IT WHEN HE TRIED TO ASSASSINATE KORO SENSEI THIS MORNING!
UH-HUH.
HE'S BEEN DEPRESSED EVER SINCE.
DON'T KNOW WHY...
IT'S NOT LIKE ANYONE ELSE HAS DONE IT.
KORO SENSEI...
OUR INVULNER-ABLE TEACHER.

RE-PORT!
HAVE YOU FIGURED OUT A WAY TO KILL HIM YET?
Ministry of Defense Special Projects Dept. Tadaomi Karasuma
IT'S IMPOSSIBLE, MR. KARASUMA.
HE'S TOO FAST.
YOU KNOW WHAT HE'S DOING TODAY AFTER SCHOOL?
HE'S GONNA DROP BY NEW YORK CITY TO CATCH A BASEBALL GAME.
HOW ARE WE SUPPOSED TO KILL A GUY WHO CAN FLY AT MACH 20?!
WOOOOOSH
I HAVE FAITH THAT YOU'LL SUCCEED...
...WHERE THE ARMIES OF THE WORLD CANNOT.
AFTER ALL, HE ALWAYS RETURNS EVERY WEEKDAY TO TEACH YOU.

IF YOU DON'T DO SOMETHING ABOUT HIM SOON...
...HE WILL DESTROY THE EARTH AFTER YOUR GRADUATION!
A disguise
KRNCH
KRNCH
Funkies
YOU SAW WHAT HE DID TO THE MOON...
...AND THAT'S JUST A LIFELESS HUNK OF ROCK!
HE'S TOO DANGEROUS TO BE LEFT ALIVE!!
AND THIS CLASSROOM IS THE ONLY PLACE IN THE WORLD WHERE WE CAN KILL HIM!!

THE STUDENTS OF CLASS E, THE CLASS OF LOSERS AND REJECTS...
...HAVE BEEN GIVEN AN OPPORTUNITY TO SAVE THE WORLD AND BECOME HEROES.
BUT WE DON'T EVEN KNOW WHY...
...KORO SENSEI WANTS TO DESTROY THE WORLD.
OR WHY...
...HE BECAME OUR TEACHER.
RING
RING
RING
RING

Sigh...
I POLISHED IT AND GOT THE SCUFF MARKS OFF IT, SUGINO.
PHNK
KORO SEN-SEI...?
WHAT ARE YOU EAT-ING?
KRNCH KRNCH
A COCONUT I BOUGHT IN HAWAII.
WANT A BITE ?
PEOPLE USUALLY DRINK THE JUICE, YOU KNOW...
THAT WAS A NICE PITCH YESTERDAY WHEN YOU TRIED TO ASSAS-SINATE ME.
YEAH, RIGHT.
THE WAY YOU MOVE I'D NEVER HAVE BEEN ABLE TO HIT YOU IN THE FIRST PLACE.
TOSS
ARE YOU ON THE BASEBALL TEAM?
I USED TO BE.
USED TO BE?

IF YOU END UP IN CLASS E...
...YOU DON'T GET TO DO SPORTS OR ANY EXTRA-CURRICULAR ACTIVITIES ANYMORE.
SINCE WE'RE HERE BECAUSE OF OUR BAD GRADES...
...WE'RE SUPPOSED TO FOCUS ON STUDYING.
YOU PROBABLY THINK THAT'S UNFAIR.
WHAT-EVER.
I DON'T CARE ANYMORE.
YOU SAW ME PITCH YESTER-DAY...
MY PITCHES SUCK.
THEY'RE TOO SLOW.

"JUNK PITCHES." OTHER TEAMS COULDN'T MISS 'EM...
...SO I GOT SCRATCHED FROM THE STARTING LINEUP.
FIGURES. I SUCK AT BASEBALL... I SUCK AT SCHOOL...
AND HERE I AM IN CLASS E!
SUGINO...
LET ME GIVE YOU SOME ADVICE.
I HAVE TO TURN IN THIS ASSIGNMENT BEFORE CLASS.
I THINK HE'S TALKING TO SUGINO.
FWIP FWIP
POP
I HOPE HE ISN'T PICKING ON HIM...
...BECAUSE OF HIS ASSAS-SINATION ATTEMPT YESTERDAY.

OH NO! IT'S WORSE THAN I THOUGHT!
WHAT ARE YOU DOING TO HIM?!
WHAT HAPPENED TO "NOT HARMING THE STUDENTS" ?!
RSTL RSTL

SUGINO...
...YOUR PITCHING FORM...
YOU MODELED IT AFTER ARITA, DIDN'T YOU? THE PITCHER WHO WENT TO THE MAJORS IN NEW YORK...
GLURGH!
MY TENTACLES...
...KNOW ALL AND SEE ALL. METAPHORICALLY SPEAKING.
PWUMP
ARI
4
THE MUSCLES IN YOUR SHOULDER AREN'T AS DEFINED AS HIS.
EVEN IF YOU COPIED HIM EXACTLY, YOU'D NEVER BE ABLE TO THROW A FASTBALL LIKE HE DOES.
H-HOW...
...CAN YOU BE SO SURE ABOUT THAT?

I CHECKED HIM OUT YESTERDAY. MY TENTACLES KNOW ALL AND SEE ALL.
From Underground
RSTL
Pitcher Arita all tangled up!
HIS TENTACLES REALLY DO KNOW ALL!
AND LOOK ...
Damn you, Tentacles!!
Arita
AFTER THAT YOU ASKED HIM FOR HIS AUTO-GRAPH?!
AND HE SIGNED ONE FOR YOU?!
GREAT ...
I KNEW IT.
I'VE GOT NOTHING.
I WOULDN'T SAY THAT.

THE FLEXIBILITY OF YOUR ELBOW AND WRIST IS REMARKABLE.
IF YOU LEARN HOW TO USE THAT TO YOUR ADVANTAGE, EVENTUALLY YOU'LL BE *BETTER* THAN ARITA!
TRUST ME...MY TENTACLES DON'T LIE.
FLOOP
THERE ISN'T JUST ONE WAY TO HAVE TALENT.
YOU JUST NEED TO FIND A METHOD THAT SUITS YOUR SKILL SET.

MY ELBOW AND WRIST...
...ARE BETTER THAN HIS...
MY...
..."TALENT"...
!!
SPLORCH
SPLORCH
KORO SENSEI!
NEW YORK...
YOU WENT ALL THE WAY THERE FOR SUGINO?
OF COURSE.
I'M HIS TEACHER.
FWIP
OTHER TEACHERS WOULDN'T DO THAT...
COME TO THINK OF IT, OTHER TEACHERS WOULDN'T DESTROY THE WORLD EITHER...

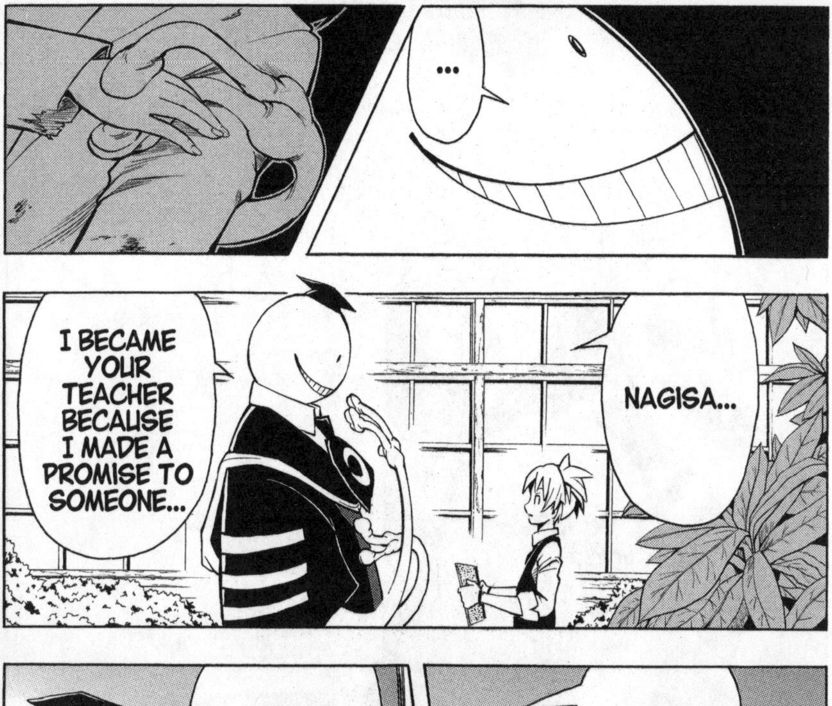
...
NAGISA...
I BECAME YOUR TEACHER BECAUSE I MADE A PROMISE TO SOMEONE...
OH, I'LL STILL DESTROY THE EARTH...
...BUT I'M YOUR TEACHER FIRST AND FOREMOST.
WSSH
WSSH
WSSH
WSSH

AND TO HELP YOU CONFRONT YOUR PROBLEMS HEAD-ON...
...MIGHT BE MORE IMPORTANT THAN DESTROYING THE EARTH.
Great!!!
96
April 23
My favorite food.
Yesterday I went to a Sushi Shop with my family to coreblate the birthday on my father (Sushi is the most favorite food of my father. and of course me!) There are a lot of attractive ingredients in the menu of the Sushi Shop. but my most favorite ingredient is octopus. its taste and texture is so wonderful that I of course ordered it yesterday. And when I ate it. my teacher appeared in my mind because his tentacle looks like the octpus. I wonder the taste of my teacher's tentacle...
celebrate
ingredients
This should be plural.
That's right!
I love sushi too!!
My favorite ingredient is botan-ebi.
No major mistakes in your grammar and you even end the last sentence with a joke. This is a wonderful diary entry!!
—Koro-Sensei
...
KORO SENSEI...
IT'S GREAT GETTING OUR ASSIGNMENTS BACK SO QUICKLY...
BUT WHAT'S WITH THE WEIRD EXTRA CREDIT QUESTIONS?
HUH ?!
I THOUGHT YOU'D LIKE THEM...
Bonus! ♡
Write a one-page essay explaining why this tentacle is just downright adorable.
IT'S MORE LIKE A PUNISH-MENT!

WELL ...
I WANT YOU TO FIND JOY—AS A STUDENT AND A WOULD-BE ASSASSIN.
SPZZZ
OR...
MNCH
MNCH
...SOMETHING LIKE THAT. YOU'LL NEVER KILL ME, BUT MAYBE THAT DOESN'T MATTER.
OUR TEACHER...
OUR TARGET...
TO TELL THE TRUTH, I REALLY DON'T THINK WE CAN KILL HIM.

SMASH
WHOA!
THAT WAS AMAZING, SUGINO!!
IT LOOKED LIKE THE BALL DISAPPEARED!!
HEH...
I'M WORKING ON A BREAKING BALL THAT MAKES FULL USE OF MY ELBOW AND WRIST.
THIS AND A CHANGE-UP MAKE FOR A GOOD ARSENAL.
IT'S STILL IMPOSSIBLY SLOW FOR KORO SENSEI THOUGH...
NAGISA...
I REFUSE TO GIVE UP...
...ON BASEBALL...
...AND ASSASSINATION.

YEAH.
SOME-HOW...
...HE MANAGES TO MOTIVATE US.
KORO SENSEI!
I WANT TO KILL YOU, SO COULD YOU PLEASE COME OUTSIDE AND PLAY CATCH?
HA HA HA! YOU DON'T GIVE UP, DO YOU?
Nagasaki Pork Belly Bun
YOU LEARN MORE THAN YOU THINK IN KORO SENSEI'S ASSASSINATION CLASSROOM!

E-11 Nagisa Shiota

- Birthday: July 20
- Height: 5' 3"
- Weight: 106 lbs.
- Favorite Subject: English
- Least Favorite Subject: Science
- Hobby/Skill: Research!
- Future Goal: None
- Personality Type: Herbivore
- If he gets the 10 billion: Find a way to grow taller

THERE HE IS!
GRNCH GRNCH
HE'S MAKING SNOW CONES FOR SNACK TIME.
YEAH... USING ICE HE JUST GOT FROM THE NORTH POLE.
CLASS 3 THE PERFECT TIME TO HELP OUT
C'MON!
WE'LL SHARE THE 10 BILLION!!
KORO SENSEI!!
FWIP
FWIP
CAN I HAVE A SNOW CONE?
Me too! Me too!
Koro Sensei!
AWW...
SNIFF
THE STUDENTS ARE FINALLY GETTING IT!
LOOK AT THOSE BIG GRINS...

SHNK
SHNK

CLASS 3
THE PERFECT TIME TO HELP OUT
AND THEY'RE ALL TRYING TO KILL ME!

SWIP
SWIP
JUST SO YOU KNOW...
SWIP
YOUR SMILES LOOKED A BIT FORCED.
NOT CONVINCING ENOUGH TO GET ME TO LET MY GUARD DOWN.
NOW GET RID OF THOSE DANGEROUS ANTI-"ME" KNIVES...
PLNK
PLNK
HEY!

...AND PUT A...
...GENUINE SMILE ON YOUR FACE BY... APPRECIATING THE BEAUTY OF THESE FLOWERS!
LOOK!!
HUH?
KORO SENSEI!!
THOSE ARE OUR FLOWERS!!
HUH?!
UM... THEY ARE?!
HOW COULD YOU, KORO SENSEI?
WE'VE BEEN GROWING THEM FOR WEEKS...
I'M SORRY... I DIDN'T KNOW...
I'LL GO GET...
WZZZP
WZZZP
...SOME NEW BULBS FOR YOU.

YOU CAN'T PLANT FLOWERS AT MACH 20!
RIGHT...
HANDLE EACH BULB WITH CARE!
OF COURSE ...
DIG
DIG
HEY...
...DOESN'T HE WANT TO DESTROY THE WORLD?
I THOUGHT SO...
...BUT I GUESS THAT DOESN'T INCLUDE TULIPS.
PFFT ...
HE'S ONLY TRYING TO MAKE HIMSELF LOOK GOOD.
NA-GISA ...
WHAT ARE YOU DOING? HOME-WORK?
SORTA. I'M WRITING DOWN KORO SENSEI'S WEAKNESSES.
IT MIGHT HELP US ASSASSI-NATE HIM SOMEDAY.
HM...

SO...
...ANY IDEA HOW?
Koro Sensei's Weakness #1
He messes up when he shows off
...
WE ARE...
...ASSASSINS.
AND THIS IS THE ASSASSINATION CLASSROOM, CLASS 3-E.
AND...
Principal's Office
TOMORROW I TAKE OVER AS THEIR P.E. TEACHER.
YOU'VE PROBABLY ALREADY BEEN INFORMED BY THE MINISTRY OF DEFENSE.

I CAN KEEP AN EYE ON HIM.
AND PROVIDE TECHNICAL AND MORAL SUPPORT FOR THE STUDENTS.
DON'T WORRY... I HAVE A TEACHING CREDENTIAL.
I TRUST YOU.
BUT THE STUDENTS' EDUCATION AND SAFETY IS MY TOP PRIORITY.
Principa
KUNUGIGAOKA JUNIOR HIGH... WHERE THE BEST OF THE BEST GO...
...AND THE WORST OF THE WORST GO TO CLASS 3-E.

THE PRINCIPAL WAS VERY UNDERSTANDING.
PLEASE...
HE'S BEING PAID A PRETTY PENNY TO LET US IN HERE.
OF COURSE HE'S UNDERSTANDING.
A MONSTER WITH ENOUGH POWER TO DESTROY THE EARTH...
THE MILITARY IS USELESS AGAINST HIM... BUT FOR SOME REASON HE WANTS TO BE A TEACHER!
THE ONLY ONES WHO KNOW ABOUT THIS...
...ARE US, THE PRINCIPAL AND CLASS 3-E.
JUST THE KIDS IN CLASS 3-E. NO ONE ELSE CAN FIND OUT.

CRAP!
THEY'LL KICK ME INTO CLASS E IF MY GRADES GET ANY WORSE.
SERIOUSLY?!
THAT SUCKS... IF YOU GO THERE YOU'RE DONE FOR.
THE ANNEX IS HORRIBLE. NO CAFETERIA... DIRTY BATHROOMS...
THE OTHER STUDENTS AND TEACHERS TREAT THE 3-E STUDENTS LIKE GARBAGE!
AND UNLESS YOU BELIEVE IN MIRACLES... YOU'LL NEVER LEAVE.
TALK ABOUT THE END CLASS...
I'D RATHER DIE THAN GET SENT THERE!
YEAH...
I'VE GOTTA STUDY HARDER SO I DON'T END UP IN 3-E!

I SEE...
...BY TREATING CLASS 3-E SO POORLY...
...THE OTHER "NORMAL" STUDENTS WORK HARDER TO FEEL SUPERIOR TO THEM—AND OUT OF FEAR OF WINDING UP THERE.
HARSH, BUT EFFECTIVE.
THIS SYSTEM GIVES US THE PERFECT SETTING FOR AN ASSAS-SINATION...
BUT IT MUST BE HELLISH...
...FOR THE BOTTOM-OF-THE-HEAP STUDENTS IN THAT CLASS!

KRNCH
KRNCH
OH, MR. KARA-SUMA!
HELLO!!
HELLO.
I'LL BE TAKING OVER AS YOUR P.E. TEACHER STARTING TOMORROW.
I HOPE WE GET ALONG.
REAL-LY?!
DOES THAT MEAN WE HAVE TO CALL YOU "COACH"?
TMP
TMP
UH...NO. BY THE WAY... WHERE IS HE?
WELL...
KORO SENSEI RUINED OUR FLOWERBED...
...AND HE WANTS TO MAKE UP FOR IT, SO...
OKAY!
I BROUGHT THE POLES AND ROPES!

...HE'S LETTING US PLAY "PIÑATA."
ZLIP
ZLIP
PA
GET HIM!!
POW
SWISH
SWISH
DAMN IT!
WE STILL CAN'T HIT HIM?!

YOU NEED TO TRY HARDER.
STAB
STAB
I'M ONLY GOING TO LET YOU DO THIS ONCE.

WHAT DO YOU THINK, NA-GISA?
YEAH ...
HE'S JUST MESSING WITH US.
TCH...
IS THIS EVEN AN ASSAS-SINATION ATTEMPT?!
BUT YOU KNOW ...
OBSERVING HIS WEAK-NESSES...
HA HA HA! WHAT'S WRONG WITH YOU, CLASS E?
IT DOESN'T GET ANY EASIER THAN THIS!
KRCK
KRCK
YOU'D THINK SOMEONE WOULD BE ABLE TO—
SNAP
OH.
FWUMP

KILL HIM, NOW!!
AAAHH!!
EEP EEP
TMP TMP
Koro Sensei's Weakness #1
He messes up when he shows off.
HUH... YOUR NOTES MIGHT COME IN HANDY.
YEAH...
LET'S SEE WHAT ELSE...
WAIT...
TIME OUT!
SWIFF
TIME OUT!
THE ROPE'S TANGLED IN MY TENTA-CLES!
STAB
Koro Sensei's Weakness #2
Panics easily.

WOOOSH
CRAP!
KADUNK
DAMN IT, HE GOT AWAY!!
BET YOU CAN'T CATCH ME UP HERE!
TOLD YOU I WAS BETTER THAN YOU, NYAAAH NYAAAH!
HUMPH...
AND WE WERE SO CLOSE!
HFF HFF HFF
Phew...
JUST FOR THAT... DOUBLE THE HOMEWORK!
THAT'S SO UNFAIR!!!!
Koro Sensei's Weakness #3 Sore loser

HE'S RUN-NING AWAY...
FOOOSH
BUT THIS WAS OUR BEST ATTEMPT YET!
自分でハンデつけたくせに
IF WE KEEP THIS UP, I KNOW WE'LL KILL HIM SOONER OR LATER!!
OOOH...
WHAT SHOULD I DO WITH THE 10 BILLION I GET FOR KILLING HIM?
JUNIOR HIGH SCHOOL STUDENTS CHEERFULLY DISCUSSING MURDER...
IF IT WEREN'T NECESSARY, IT WOULD BE CREEPY.
NA-GISA...
WHAT DO YOU THINK?
CAN WE KILL KORO SENSEI?

WE'LL KILL HIM.
WE JUST HAVE TO GO ALL OUT.
FUNNY THING IS...
...OUT OF ALL THE KIDS AT THIS SCHOOL...
...THE ONES IN CLASS E ARE THE MOST OPTIMISTIC.
ZOOOOP
OOF

THAT'S EVERY-THING...
TO PREVENT A PANIC, YOU ARE FORBIDDEN FROM SPEAKING ABOUT THIS.
IF YOU DO, WE WILL BE FORCED TO ERASE YOUR MEMORY.
FREAKY ...!
THE OTHER STUDENTS IN CLASS E HAVE ALREADY BEEN BRIEFED...
...AND ARE ALREADY WORKING ON THEIR MISSION.
ONCE YOUR SUSPENSION IS OVER...
...
...WE ASSUME YOU WILL DO THE SAME.

HEY...
CAN THIS RUBBER KNIFE REALLY HURT HIM?
BOING
IT CAN.
IT'S HARMLESS TO HUMANS BUT HIGHLY EFFECTIVE AGAINST THE TARGET.
BOING
HM...
COOL. HUMAN OR NOT...
SHUNK
WANTED
...YOU HAVE NO IDEA...
...HOW LONG I'VE BEEN ITCHING TO KILL A TEACHER...

Kunugigaoka Junior High Bulletin Board

School Policies for the Kunugigaoka Junior High Special Placement Class.

For students who have been transferred to the Special Placement Class (Class 3-E) due to poor academic performance.

- All classes will be held in building 3-E. At no time will students be allowed to enter the main school building without special permission.
- To avoid distraction from their studies, students are forbidden to take part in extracurricular activities.
- All other classes receive priority consideration for special activities over Class 3-E.
- If students put in the effort and earn good grades in 3-E, they will be allowed to return to their previous class.
- Students who are still in 3-E at the end of the second trimester will not be permitted to graduate.
- Students transferred into 3-E must abide by the above school policies and are hereby advised that they will be strictly enforced.

IN OTHER WORDS, CLASS E IS HOPELESS!!

Kunugigaoka School Mascot

Kunudon

CLASS 4 TIME TO GET DOWN TO WORK

This is Koro Sensei
Sucker
Sticky. Can even pick up a toothpick from a smooth floor.
Head
Super smart. Can teach most subjects by himself. Has a sweet tooth.
Tuna Dissection Demonstration
Next show: 3:00
Fresh Fish
King Crab
Horse Mackerel
Sea Bream
Slime
Can secrete a slippery slime from his body at will. It helps lower air resistance, allowing for nearly silent supersonic flight.
Tentacles
Even he has no idea how many tentacles are hidden beneath his robes.

One, two...
Three, four...
Five, six, seven, eight...
AH, HOW I LOVE THE SOUND OF STUDENTS PLAYING OUT ON THE SPORTS FIELD.
IT'S SO PEACE-FUL...
Koro Sensei
One, two...
Three, four...
Five, six, seven, eight...
IF ONLY THEY WEREN'T WIELDING WEAPONS...
SWISH
SWISH
SWISH
AGAIN, FROM ATTACK STANCE ONE!!
AND KEEP YOUR BALANCE!!

I THOUGHT I TOLD YOU TO TAKE A BREAK.
Why are you weaaring that?
I'M THE NEW P.E. TEACHER.
YOU'RE NOT LISTENING, ARE YOU?
LEAVE US ALONE. GO PLAY IN THE SANDBOX OR SOMETHING.
WHY ARE YOU SO MEAN, MR. KARASUMA?
THE STUDENTS LOVED MY P.E. CLASS!
NOT REALLY...
LIKE THE OTHER DAY...
...YOUR SIDE-STEPPING EXERCISE ...
OKAY, THIS IS REALLY SIMPLE...
I'LL DEMON-STRATE HOW IT'S DONE FIRST.

Koro Sensei
Koro Sensei
Koro Sensei
WE'LL START WITH HIGH-SPEED VISUAL CLONING.
ONCE YOU GET THE HANG OF THAT, WE'LL ADD IN CAT'S CRADLE.
VISUAL CLONING?!
IT WAS PRETTY COOL...
YEAH, BUT I WANT TO LEARN P.E. FOR HUMAN BODIES!
WHA...?!

Sniff
Sniff
oro Sensei
FINALLY SOME PEACE AND QUIET.
LET'S GET ON WITH THE CLASS.
WHY ARE WE DOING THIS, MR. KARASUMA?
ESPECIALLY WITH OUR TARGET RIGHT IN FRONT OF US...WATCHING OUR EVERY MOVE.
ASSASSINATION IS A SKILL LIKE ANY OTHER.
THE BETTER YOU KNOW THE BASICS, THE BETTER YOU'LL PERFORM.
HMM...
FOR EXAMPLE... LET'S SEE...
ISOGAI!
MAE-HARA!
TRY AND HIT ME WITH THAT RUBBER KNIFE.

WHAT ...?
ARE YOU SURE?
IT WON'T HURT HUMANS.
IF YOU HIT ME, I'LL LET CLASS OUT EARLY.
THE TWO OF US? AT THE SAME TIME?
UM...
UH...
TMP
OKAY!
JAB
JINK
AHH...
THAT IT?
HAI-YA!

BA
F
WIFF
WFF
SEE WHAT YOU CAN DO...
WIFF
BAMP
WIFF
SMAK
SWISH
...WITH A LITTLE TRAINING?
WOW...
DAMN!

YANK
FLIP
WHOA!
ACK!
IF YOU CAN'T HIT ME...
...HOW ARE YOU GOING TO HIT SOMEONE WHO CAN MOVE AT MACH 20?

HURMM...
WE MUST HAVE BORED HIM.
HE CHANGED HIS OUTFIT, MADE GREEN TEA, AND BUILT A SAND CASTLE...
SHOW-OFF...
GRIN
HMPF
IF YOU CAN IMPROVE YOUR SKILLS ENOUGH TO HIT ME...
...YOU'LL BETTER YOUR CHANCES OF HITTING HIM.
KNIVES, PISTOLS, SNIPER RIFLES, ASSAULT WEAPONS... THE BASICS OF ASSASSINATION...
YOU'RE GOING TO LEARN THEM ALL IN MY CLASS!
RING RING RING RING

KRNCH
...
MR. KARASUMA'S KINDA SCARY...BUT HE'S COOL.
YEAH!
I THINK I'M GOING TO ENJOY P.E. FROM NOW ON.
MR. KARA-SUMA...
YOU'RE TRYING TO WIN THEM OVER, AREN'T YOU?
WHAT KIND OF A JOKE IS THIS?
SKWEEK
RSTL
IF I REMEMBER YOUR CONTRACT CORRECTLY...
"THE SCHOOL DISTRICT MAY ADD EXTRA TEACH-ERS..."
"...TO PROVIDE ASSISTANCE AT ANY TIME IF THE NEED ARISES."
!
THNK

MY JOB IS TO OVERSEE THESE ASSASSINS...
TINK
...UNTIL THEY ASSAS-SINATE YOU.
I HAVE A NAME...
GRIN
THE STUDENTS GAVE IT TO ME. PLEASE CALL ME "KORO SENSEI."
WE HAVE A TEST AFTER THIS...
IT WOULD BE AWE-SOME IF P.E. WAS OUR LAST CLASS FOR THE DAY!
HUH?
WSSH
HH
WS
SH
LOOK WHO'S HERE...

SSSH
WSS
KARMA...
YOU'RE BACK!
WSSH
HIYA.
LONG TIME NO SEE, NAGISA.
WHOA!
SO THAT'S KORO SENSEI?
HE LOOKS LIKE AN OCTOPUS. FREAKY.
FWIP

FWIP
HMM...
FWIP
KARMA AKABANE...?
YOU WERE SUPPOSED TO COME TO CLASS THIS MORNING.
BEING LATE ON YOUR FIRST DAY BACK FROM SUSPENSION DOESN'T LOOK GOOD.
HEH HEH ...
I GOT USED TO SLEEPING IN.
KIDDING! SORRY I'M LATE.
IT'S NICE TO MEET YOU, KORO SENSEI!!
NICE TO MEET YOU TOO.
I LOOK FORWARD TO A PRODUCTIVE YEAR TOGETHER.
GRP

FSS
SSS
!
SNKT

YOINK
FSSSS
WOW...
YOU ARE FAST.
AND THEY WEREN'T LYING WHEN THEY SAID THIS WOULD HURT YOU.
EVEN LITTLE TINY SLIVERS LIKE THIS.
FSSSS

I CAN'T BELIEVE...
...YOU FELL FOR THE OLDEST TRICK IN THE BOOK!
AND LOOK AT YOU WAY OVER THERE. YOU SCARED? BWAK BWAK BWAK...
TMP
THIS IS THE FIRST TIME...
...ANYONE HAS INFLICTED DAMAGE ON KORO SENSEI!!
TMP
TMP
SCHLORP
"KORO SENSEI..." THAT'S A PLAY ON "KORO SENAI" ISN'T IT...? "CAN'T KILL"...
TMP
!

YOU KNOW...
...I THINK THEY GOT YOUR NAME WRONG.

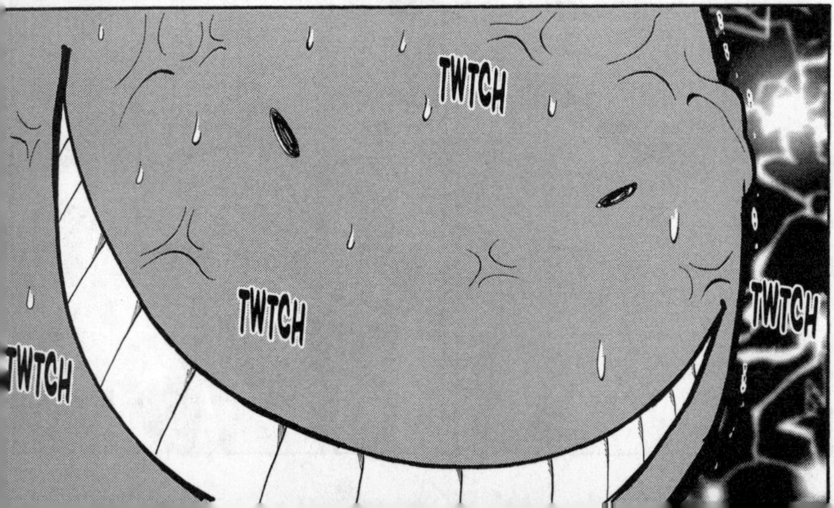
TWTCH
TWTCH
TWTCH
TWTCH

NA-GISA...
I HAVEN'T BEEN IN CLASS E THAT LONG, SO... WHO'S THAT GUY?
WHAT'S HIS STORY?
WELL ...
WE WERE IN THE SAME CLASS MY FIRST AND SECOND YEAR...
BUT HE KEPT GETTING SUSPENDED FOR FIGHTING.
ORDINARY TEACHERS COULDN'T HANDLE HIM. I GUESS THEY FINALLY SENT HIM TO 3-E.
BUT KNOWING KARMA ...
...HE'LL BE AT THE HEAD OF THE CLASS IN NO TIME.
HUH ?
WHAT DO YOU MEAN?
KLCK

WHEN IT COMES TO WEAPONRY, BATTLE TACTICS, AND SNEAK ATTACKS...
...KARMA IS PROBABLY THE BEST OUT OF ALL OF US.
DON'T RUN TOO FAR, KORO SENSEI.
TING
TING
TING
I DON'T NEED THE EXERCISE...I JUST NEED TO KILL YOU.

TADAOMI KARASUMA

- BIRTHDAY: AUGUST 15 (28 YEARS OLD)
- HEIGHT: 5' 11"
- WEIGHT: 187 LBS.
- CAREER HISTORY: 1ST AIRBORNE BRIGADE→ INTER-SERVICES INTELLIGENCE → CONTINGENCY SPECIAL PROJECTS DEPARTMENT→ CLASS 3-E PE TEACHER.
- HOBBY/SKILLS: GENERAL COMBAT
- MOTTO: DO THE POSSIBLE AND CARRY OUT THE IMPOSSIBLE.
- FAVORITE ANIMAL: DOG
- DOGS: THEY BARK LIKE CRAZY WHEN HE PASSES.

CLASS 5 MAKING TIME FOR KARMA

BOING
BOING
WHAT'S KORO SENSEI DOING?
BOING
I DON'T KNOW...
BOING
SKRTCH SKRTCH
MAYBE HE'S PUNCH-ING THE WALL?
BOING
AH...
HE'S MAD BECAUSE KARMA GOT THE BETTER OF HIM.
BOING
BOING
IF THAT'S AS HARD AS HE CAN HIT THAT'S PRETTY SAD.
BOING
Koro Sensei's Weakness #4
Weak punches.
THE WALL SUR-RENDERS, KORO SENSEI!!
WHAT ABOUT OUR TEST?!
WHAT? OH! SORRY!

HEY, KARMA...
YOU DON'T WANT TO GET THAT MONSTER MAD, YOU KNOW.
TERASAKA KNOWS ALL ABOUT MAKING HIM MAD.
HEH.
OF COURSE I MADE HIM MAD. I ALMOST KILLED HIM...
HEY, TERA-SAKA...
DIDJA WET YOUR PANTS AFTER YOU PISSED HIM OFF?
WHA...?
SLAM
I DID NOT!! THAT'S...
YOU WANNA PIECE OF ME?!
HEY, YOU TWO!!
QUIET DURING THE TEST!!
TELL IT TO YOUR TENTA-CLES!
TSK TSK

SORRY, KORO SENSEI.
I'M DONE WITH MY TEST NOW.
SO I'LL JUST SIT HERE AND EAT MY GELATO.
YOU KNOW YOU'RE NOT ALLOWED TO EAT IN CLASS.
WHERE DID YOU GET THAT, ANYWAY?
!!
HEY! THAT...
THAT'S MY GELATO!! I BOUGHT IT IN ITALY YESTERDAY !!
IT'S YOURS?!
I FOUND IT IN THE FREEZER IN THE FACULTY ROOM.
OOPS. MY BAD.
"MY BAD"?!
I HAD TO FLY THROUGH THE STRATOSPHERE TO KEEP IT FROM MELTING ON MY WAY BACK!! AND THE STRATOSPHERE IS COLD!!

HM...
SO WHAT ARE YOU GONNA DO ABOUT IT?
SQUISHY-PUNCH ME?
"SQUISHY-PUNCH"?
NO. I'M JUST GOING TO EAT WHAT'S LEFT OF MY GELATO!!
FLOOP
...
!!
FSSSSS
FSSSSS
WHEN DID HE PUT THOSE ON THE FLOOR?!
SKTTL
ANTI-ME BB'S...

HA HA!
YOU FELL FOR IT AGAIN.
PAPOW
PAPOW
PAPOW
!
PAPOW
I'M GOING TO KEEP THIS UP, YOU KNOW.
YOU THINK I CARE IF I DISRUPT YOUR CLASS?
SKRTCH
IF YOU DON'T LIKE IT...
...KILL MY PARENTS... KILL WHOEVER...
...

BUT ONCE YOU DO...
...YOU WON'T BE A TEACHER ANYMORE...
...YOU'LL BE A MONSTER.
SPLORCH
I'VE BEEN WANTING...
...TO KILL A TEACHER.
HERE'S MY TEST.
I KNOW I ACED IT.
!
SEE YOU, KORO SENSEI...
SHFF
LET'S PLAY AGAIN TOMORROW!

KARMA IS REALLY SMART...
LIKE RIGHT NOW...
HE KNOWS THERE'S A LINE KORO SENSEI CAN'T CROSS...
...
...AND HE'S TRYING TO PUSH KORO SENSEI RIGHT TO THAT EDGE.
THE SAD THING IS...
...HE DOES THAT WITH EVERY-BODY—
...PUSHES THEM RIGHT TO THE EDGE...
FWIP
FWIP
HE DOESN'T TRUST ANYONE.

HMPH...
THANKS TO HIM, I HAVE TO GO GET A NEW GELATO.
WEEEZZZZZZZZZZ
Test: History
Karma Akabane
100
HE'S SMART. AND HE'S RIGHT...
I CAN'T KILL OR HARM HIM...
...IF I WANT TO KEEP WORKING AS A TEACHER.
SO...
...WHAT SHOULD I DO WITH HIM...?

Kunugigaoka Station
BYE, NAGISA!
BYE!
SEE YOU TOMORROW!
HEY...
IT'S NAGISA.
FREAK FITS RIGHT INTO 3-E.
OF COURSE... HE'S A LOSER.
I DON'T THINK HE'S EVER COMING BACK TO OUR CLASS.
GUESS WHAT!
I HEARD AKABANE GOT SENT THERE AFTER HIS SUSPENSION.
WHOA! THAT SUCKS!
I'D RATHER DIE THAN END UP IN 3-E!

REALLY?
YOU'D RATHER DIE?
SHATTR
THEN HOW ABOUT RIGHT NOW?
AKABANE!!
DASH
AAAH!!
HA HA HA... THEY SERIOUSLY THOUGHT I WAS GONNA KILL THEM.
KAR-MA...
I DON'T HAVE TIME TO GET SUSPENDED AGAIN...
...NOW THAT I HAVE A NEW TOY TO PLAY WITH...

SO, NAGISA...
...THERE'S SOMETHING I'VE BEEN MEANING TO ASK YOU.
YOU KNOW A LOT ABOUT KORO SENSEI, RIGHT?
UM... I GUESS...
A LITTLE BIT...
WOULD HE GET MAD...
...IF I CALLED HIM AN OCTOPUS?
AN... OCTOPUS...?
HMM. PROBABLY NOT...
HE MIGHT EVEN TAKE IT AS A COMPLIMENT.
HE SIGNS HIS TESTS WITH AN OCTOPUS.
sodium
Octopus X!!
A lot of students make this mistake. Be careful!!
AND HE USES AN OCTOPUS AVATAR WHEN HE PLAYS VIDEO GAMES...
SHUF SHUF
AND THE OTHER DAY, HE DUG A HOLE IN THE SCHOOLYARD AND...

HELP! I'M STUCK IN AN OCTOPUS POT!
HE MADE AN OCTOPUS JOKE?!
THE OCTOPUS IS BECOMING HIS TRADEMARK.
It was funny, though.
YEAH YEAH ...
HMM...
I JUST GOT THIS CRAZY IDEA...
GRIN
急行
通過します.
KARMA ...
WHAT ARE YOU UP TO...?

HNNNK HNNNK
I AM...
...REALLY HAPPY. REALLY HAPPY.
I WAS AFRAID HE WAS GOING TO TURN OUT TO BE JUST SOME WEIRD MONSTER...
...BUT HE ACTUALLY IS A TEACHER. A REAL TEACHER.
RMMMMMMMMM
I CAN'T BELIEVE I GET TO KILL A TEACHER WITH MY OWN HANDS!
IT'S PAYBACK TIME! AFTER WHAT HAPPENED WITH THE LAST ONE...
...?

CAN MY DAY GET ANY WORSE?
I DIDN'T HAVE ENOUGH MONEY TO BUY A GELATO.
AND I WON'T GET ANY MORE TILL PAYDAY.
GUESS I'M EATING IN TONIGHT.
THERE ARE SOME COOKING UTENSILS IN THE STOREROOM I CAN USE...
GOOD MORNING.
SHFF
...
UM...
WHAT'S THE MATTER, EVERYONE?

I AM SO SORRY.
I THOUGHT IT WAS YOU...AND I KILLED IT.
I'LL THROW IT AWAY FOR YOU, IF YOU HAND IT TO ME.
...?
OKAY.
SPLORCH

COME ON, KORO SENSEI...
I DON'T NEED TO KILL YOU JUST YET...
I'LL START OFF BY...
...MAKING YOU WISH YOU WERE DEAD!
FZZ Z ZZ ZZF ZFFF
WHA ...?!

WOOSH
WSSSPF
LET ME SHOW YOU SOMETHING, KARMA...
THE SPEED OF MY DRILL TENTACLES...
VROOOOOSH
AND THE FIREPOWER OF THE MISSILE I TOOK FROM THE NAVY.

FZZZZ
ZZZZZ
ZZZZZ
ZZZ
ZZP
PPP
I WILL NEVER...
...LET AN ASSASSIN GET AWAY SCOT-FREE.
SWISH

!!
YOU LOOK PALE. YOU SKIPPED BREAKFAST, DIDN'T YOU?
AACK ...
WFF WFF
OCTOPUS DUMPLINGS COOKED AT MACH 20!
IT'S THE MOST IMPORTANT MEAL OF THE DAY! BREAKFAST, THAT IS.
WFF WFF
...
KARMA, IT IS MY JOB...
...TO POLISH YOU...
...AN ASSASSIN'S BLADE THAT HAS BECOME RUSTY AND DULL.

COME AT ME WITH EVERYTHING YOU'VE GOT ALL DAY LONG.
AND I'LL KEEP POLISHING YOU...
!!
...BY THE END OF CLASS TODAY...
...YOUR BODY AND SPIRIT WILL BE SPARKLY CLEAN.

Never cut corners.

Sure thing.
I'll take the freshest looking cephalopod.

That is the secret to harassment.

-1ST PERIOD: MATH-
NO MATTER HOW HARD YOU TRY, YOU'RE ALWAYS LEFT WITH THIS NUMBER!
SO WHAT DO YOU DO...?
Which one?
DON'T WORRY! I'LL SHOW YOU!
SCRTCH
SCRTCH
SCRTCH
LET'S SOLVE IT TOGETHER.
...
KLCK
CLASS 6 IT'S TIME TO MAKE A CHOICE

CLASS 6
IT'S TIME TO MAKE A CHOICE
NOW ...
...ADD THESE ALL UP TOGETH-ER...
AND THEN... TO OUR SUR-PRISE...
TA-DAH!
KLNCH
KLNCH
KLNCH
KLNCH
YOUR ANSWER!
WAY TOO SLOW, KARMA.
Solved.
I MEAN, REALLY...
I HAD ENOUGH TIME TO DO YOUR NAILS TOO. YOU LIKE THEM?
!!

-4TH PERIOD: HOME ECONOMICS-
HAS YOUR GROUP FINISHED, FUWA?
HMM, I DON'T KNOW...
IT'S TOO BITTER...
LET ME TRY IT.
I KNOW...
WHY DON'T YOU MAKE IT AGAIN?
AH!
GET RID OF THIS BATCH FIRST.
SMAK

WHAT THE-?!
ALWAYS WEAR AN APRON IN THE KITCHEN, KARMA.
AND DON'T WORRY ABOUT THE SOUP.
I GOT IT ALL WITH AN EYEDROPPER.
ZUP ZUP ZUP ZUP ZUP ZUP
I EVEN ADDED A PINCH OF SUGAR.
HEY...
...IT'S PERFECT NOW!!
Ha ha...
snkr

IMPOS-SIBLE...
-5TH PERIOD: LITERATURE-
KORO SENSEI HAS A TON OF WEAKNESSES.
BUT ...
HE MESSES UP A LOT...
...AND WHEN HE PANICS HIS REACTION TIME SLOWS WAY DOWN...
...NO MATTER HOW GOOD KARMA IS...
RSTL
"...AND EVEN AS THOSE THOUGHTS PASSED THROUGH MY MIND..."

POINK
"...THE RED FROG FAILED AND RETURNED..."
"...I BEGAN TO GROW BORED..."
SPRITZ
COMB
COMB
Hair
"...SO I PICKED A COUPLE PEBBLES OFF THE ROAD AND..."
EXCERPT FROM KENSAKU SHIMAKI'S "THE RED FROG."
ASSASSINATION IS LIKE A NEVER-ENDING GAME...
RING RING RING RING
...WHEN HE'S ON HIS GUARD.

WOOOOSH
NIBBL NIBBL
KAR-MA...
THERE'S NO RUSH. WE'LL KILL HIM TOGETHER... EVENTUALLY.
ONCE KORO SENSEI'S ON TO YOU...
...IT'S IMPOSSIBLE TO KILL HIM BY YOURSELF, NO MATTER WHAT YOU DO.
HE'S NO ORDINARY TEACHER, AFTER ALL.
...
TEACHER, HUH...

AKABANE!!
YOUR ATTITUDE... NEEDS WORK...
IT HAS THE POTENTIAL TO GET YOU INTO A LOT OF TROUBLE...
BUT AS LONG AS YOU DO WHAT'S RIGHT...
...I'LL BACK YOU UP!!
HELL NO...
I WANNA KILL HIM MYSELF.
I DON'T WANT HIM DROPPING DEAD ANYWHERE ELSE.
SURE ...
KARMA...
I SURE DID A LOT OF WORK ON YOUR HAIR TODAY.
FLOOP

BUT IF YOU WANT TO KEEP ON TRYING TO KILL ME...
...I HAVE PLENTY MORE HAIRSPRAY AND NAIL POLISH.
CAN I ASK YOU SOME-THING?
YOU'RE A TEACHER, RIGHT, KORO SENSEI?
YES.
I AM.
WOOSH
HEH.
AND TEACH-ERS...
...PROTECT THEIR STUDENTS—WITH THEIR LIVES, YEAH?
OF COURSE.
THAT'S WHAT TEACHERS DO.
KLCK
THAT'S GOOD TO HEAR.
THEN I'VE GOT YOU...

...TEACH!
JUMP
COME HELP ME AND...
...I'LL SHOOT AND KILL YOU.

LET ME FALL TO MY DOOM AND...
...YOU'RE DEAD AS A TEACHER.

FREAKY...
YOUR LIFE REALLY DOES FLASH BEFORE YOUR EYES...
YOU OKAY?
3-E
3-E... AS IN THAT CLASS?
THEY PICKED ON YOU BECAUSE OF SOMETHING STUPID LIKE THAT?
HUH?
OF COURSE I WAS IN THE RIGHT.
WHAT COULD POSSIBLY BE WRONG WITH PROTECTING A STUDENT FROM A BULLY?

NO, AKABANE.
YOU WERE CLEARLY IN THE WRONG.
WHAT?!
ARE YOU NUTS?!
YOU BEAT UP THE SCHOOL VALEDIC-TORIAN! YOU CAN'T DO THAT!
HUH?
WAIT A MINUTE...
YOU BEAT UP A STUDENT WITH A FUTURE—A BRIGHT FUTURE—JUST BECAUSE HE PICKED ON A STUDENT IN CLASS E!! CLASS E.
Jeez...
AND WHO'S GOING TO BE HELD RESPONSIBLE IF THIS SCREWS UP HIS HIGH SCHOOL PLACEMENT EXAMS? ME!
YOU SAID YOU'D ALWAYS BE ON MY SIDE...
YOU TOLD ME YOU HAD MY BACK...
HE'S...DYING.

IT'S LIKE HE'S DYING INSIDE...
I SUPPORTED YOU BECAUSE YOU GOT GOOD GRADES.
KRMBL
BUT IF YOU'RE GOING TO SCREW ME OVER...
KRMBL
... DAMAGE MY REPUTATION...
KRMBL
WELL, SURPRISE! I GOT YOU A TRANSFER!
CONGRATULATIONS, AKABANE.
FROM THIS DAY ON, YOU GET TO BE A MEMBER OF YOUR BELOVED CLASS E.
THAT WAS WHEN I FIGURED OUT A PERSON COULD BE DEAD AND ALIVE AT THE SAME TIME.
ONCE I SAW WHAT HE WAS INSIDE...
...THAT TEACHER WAS DEAD TO ME.
KORO SENSEI !!
ONE WAY OR THE OTHER!!
WHICH "DEATH" ARE YOU GONNA CHOOSE?!

ZZPPPPPFFFF
WHAT ...?!
FLWUMP
KA

KARMA...
I TAKE MY HAT OFF TO YOU FOR THIS BRILLIANTLY STRATEGIZED ASSASSINATION ATTEMPT.
IF I SAVED YOU AT SUPERSONIC SPEED, YOUR BODY COULDN'T HANDLE IT.
BUT IF I SAVED YOU SLOWLY, YOU'D SHOOT ME.
POP
SO...
...I DECIDED TO BECOME A LITTLE STICKY.
SPLITCH
DAMN IT...
IT'S ANYTHING GOES WITH THOSE TENTACLES!!
NOW YOU CAN'T SHOOT ME! AHAHAHA-HAHAHA...
ACK...
OH, AND BY THE WAY...

ABANDONING YOU IS NOT AN OPTION.
JUMP OFF CLIFFS ANY TIME YOU WISH—I'LL CATCH YOU.
...
HEH...
THIS IS HOPELESS.
HE WON'T DIE AND I CAN'T KILL HIM...

AT LEAST...
...NOT AS A TEACHER...
KARMA...
I CAN'T BELIEVE YOU DID THAT!
WELL...
IT WAS THE BEST PLAN I HAD YET...
OKAY... MAYBE NOT THE BEST...
OUT OF IDEAS AL-READY?
THAT'S A SHAME...
OOH, LOOK AT ALL THE PRODUCT I HAVEN'T HAD A CHANCE TO USE ON YOU YET...
I GUESS YOU'RE ACTUALLY MORE OF A SLACKER THAN I THOUGHT.

...
I STILL WANT TO KILL HIM.
Hmph
BUT...
I FEEL DIFFERENT ABOUT IT NOW.
SLICE
I'LL KILL YOU...
...TOMORROW OR SO...
HE'S READY FOR CLEAN AND HEALTHY ASSAS-SINATIONS NOW.
DOESN'T NEED AS MUCH POLISHING UP.
GRIN

LET'S GO HOME, NAGISA.
WE CAN GET A BITE TO EAT ON THE WAY.
HEY!
THAT'S MY WALLET!!
YEAH? WELL, YOU...
...SHOULDN'T LEAVE IT LYING AROUND THE FACULTY ROOM.
GIVE IT BACK!!
SURE.
BUT IT'S EMPTY!!
ANY ASSASSIN WHO TRIES TO KILL KORO SENSEI...
...GETS SPARKLING CLEAN—MORE THAN THEY BARGAINED FOR.
IT WAS JUST NICKELS AND DIMES. I THREW THEM IN A DONATION BOX.
WHAT?! YOU, YOU... ROBIN HOOD!!
THAT'S THE ASSASSINATION CLASSROOM FOR YOU.
HEY, HOW SHOULD WE KILL HIM TOMORROW...?

Assassination Will Keep Us Together

He'll do a 100 K run in 21 seconds for charity on TV.
245

...AND THAT'S HOW YOU GET THE ARTIFICIAL COLOR OUT OF SNACKS...
I'LL TAKE THESE, THANK YOU....
Mc ti-tei
Pokil
RING RING RING RING
HE JUST DOESN'T WANT TO WAIT TILL PAYDAY TO GET SNACKS.
Hey! We bought those!
WAIT... WHY IS HE DRAWING A SALARY IF HE'S PLANNING TO DESTROY THE WORLD...?
COOKies
FWIP
LUB DUB
LUB DUB
CLASS 7 TIME FOR A REFRESHING DRINK
UM...
KORO SENSEI... YEAH... UM...

CLASS 7 TIME FOR A REFRESHING DRINK
IT'S POISON!!
PLEASE DRINK IT!!
FWUMP
OKUDA...
...THAT WAS... HONEST.
UH...
UMM ...

I'M NOT GOOD AT SURPRISE ATTACKS LIKE EVERYONE ELSE...
BUT...
...I LOVE CHEMISTRY! AND I REALLY PUT MY HEART AND SOUL INTO THIS...
OKUDA...
WHAT KIND OF IDIOT WOULD DRINK THAT AFTER YOU—
化学
WOW!
IS THAT SO?
LEMME TRY IT!
GULP
HE DRANK IT!!
TRMBL
THIS IS...
TRMBL
THIS...
TRMBL

PLOINK
HE GREW HORNS!
...SODIUM HYDROX-IDE.
HARMFUL TO HUMANS BUT NOT TO ME.
OH ...
YOU'VE GOT TWO MORE.
I'LL GIVE THEM A TRY TOO.
UM ... YES ...!
Unnh.
URrgh.
GYURGS...

FLAP
NOW HE GREW WINGS!!
ACTUALLY LOOKS KINDA COOL.
AND THE LAST ONE...
THALLIUM ACETATE.
WHATTYA THINK WILL HAPPEN NOW?!
HOW WILL HE TRANSFORM THIS TIME?!
LUB DUB
LUB DUB
LUB DUB

UMM...
TALK ABOUT EXPRESSION-LESS!!
AQUA REGIA...
THAT'S ALL THEY DID TO ME, HUH?
UHH ...
YOU LOOK LIKE AN EMOTICON !!
HE DOES!
"DON'T HATE ME BECAUSE I'M BEAUTI-FUL."
WHAT'S HE TALKING ABOUT?!

NOW, OKUDA...
...YOU KNOW I CAN'T ALLOW A STUDENT TO CONCOCT DANGEROUS POISONS WITHOUT SUPERVISION.
RIGHT...
I APOLOGIZE...
DO YOU HAVE TIME AFTER SCHOOL TODAY?
WE CAN RESEARCH A POISON THAT CAN KILL ME—TOGETHER!
UM...
OKAY!
SHE'S GOING TO...
...MAKE POISON... *WITH* THE POISON'S TARGET?
YEAH...
I DON'T SEE THAT ENDING WELL...

NOW ADD THE ETHANOL TO IT.
AND BE CAREFUL NOT TO BREATHE IN THE FUMES.
OKAY!
YOUR GRADES IN CHEMISTRY ARE EXCELLENT, BUT...
YEAH, I KNOW...
I GET TERRIBLE GRADES IN EVERYTHING ELSE.
IT'S NO WONDER I WAS TRANS-FERRED TO CLASS E.
ESPE-CIALLY IN...
...WRITING.
I JUST CAN'T...
...FIND THE RIGHT WORDS TO SAY WHAT I FEEL!
the wander sad exp emptiness the hum world A star fa down from the sky.
I NEVER KNOW WHAT THE RIGHT ANSWER IS!
...
BUT... WITH MATH AND SCIENCE...
...THERE'S IS A RIGHT ANSWER.

SO I...
...DON'T NEED BEAUTIFUL WORDS...
...OR TO THINK ABOUT COMPLICATED EMOTIONS...
RIGHT...
SCRBBL SCRBBL
BUT I HAVE...
...A LITTLE HOMEWORK FOR YOU.
Step ①
NH4Cl 35% + Na2S2
BAM
THIS IS...
...THE POISON HE ASKED YOU TO MAKE?
IT IS!!
HE SAID THIS POISON WOULD BE MOST EFFECTIVE!!

HE EVEN DREW A MANGA ABOUT HOW TO STORE IT PROPERLY.
THAT'S OUR KORO SENSEI... ALWAYS TRYING TO HELP.
Storing It Wrong!
Storing It Right!
Argh!
I THINK HE REALLY GETS ME.
IT'S EASIER TO UNDERSTAND AS A MANGA. I CAN FOCUS ON MY STRENGTHS.
OH.
THERE HE IS. WHY DON'T YOU GIVE IT TO HIM?
SHFF
I CAN'T WAIT!
KORO SENSEI! HERE...!
WELL DONE...
I'LL TAKE IT RIGHT AWAY.
GULP
GULP
GULP

DUB
LUB
AHA HAHA HAHA HA...
OKUDA...
LUB DUB
LUB DUB
...THANKS TO YOUR POTION...
...I CAN MOVE ON TO THE NEXT LEVEL.
LUB DUB
UM...
WHAT DO YOU MEAN...?
SHA
TTR
GYUUUUUURGH!
TING!!

Phew.
HE MELTED!!
WHAT I ACTUALLY HAD YOU MAKE...
...WAS A CONCOCTION THAT WOULD TURN ME INTO A LIQUID—OBVIOUSLY.
SPLORP
TNK

AND NOW THAT I'M A LIQUID...
...I CAN LEAK THROUGH THE SMALLEST OF SPACES!!
TO TOP IT OFF, I'M STILL AS FAST AS BEFORE!!
LET'S SEE IF YOU CAN KILL ME NOW!!
SWOOSH
PING PING
PING PING
PING
SPLORCH
SWISH
WZZZ
HEY...
IT WAS HARD ENOUGH BEFORE!!
THERE'S NO WAY WE CAN HIT YOU WHEN YOU KEEP HIDING IN THE CEILING AND UNDERNEATH THE FLOOR-BOARDS!!
I NEVER KILLED A LIQUID METAL SLIME IN THAT GAME EITHER...
FWIP
FWIP
FWIP
FWIP
FWIP

OKUDA...
KORO SENSEI TOLD YOU THAT WAS POISON?
UM ...
La la la
SO YOU...
...LIED TO ME, KORO SENSEI?!
OKUDA ...
YOU NEED GOOD COMMUNICATION SKILLS TO DECEIVE PEOPLE IF YOU'RE TO HAVE ANY HOPE OF ASSASSINAT-ING THEM.
WHAT...?
NO MATTER HOW GOOD YOU ARE AT CREATING POISONS...
Poison
Poison
...IF YOU JUST HAND THEM OVER...
...YOUR TARGET IS ONLY GOING TO USE THEM AGAINST YOU.
Poison

NA-GISA...
HOW WOULD YOU POISON ME?
ME?
HMM...
I'D PROBABLY MIX THE POISON INTO YOUR JUICE...
...AND OFFER IT TO YOU SAYING IT WAS A SPECIAL HOMEMADE DRINK I MADE...
...I GUESS.
EX-ACTLY.
IN ORDER TO DECEIVE SOMEONE, YOU NEED TO UNDERSTAND HOW THEY FEEL, WHAT MOTIVATES THEM.
YOU NEED TO INTERPRET... COMMUNI-CATE...
THE SKILLS YOU DEVELOP THROUGH READING AND WRITING...
...ARE NECESSARY FOR A GOOD POISONING.

YOUR CHEMISTRY SKILLS WILL COME IN HANDY IN THE FUTURE.
The effect wore off.
BUT YOU'LL NEED TO WORK ON YOUR COMMUNICA-TION SKILLS...
...BECAUSE ONE WAY OR ANOTHER... YOU'RE GOING TO HAVE TO EXPLAIN YOUR WORK SO THAT OTHERS CAN UNDERSTAND IT.
SCHLORP
YES...
I UNDER-STAND.
HEH HEH ...
THIS ISN'T JUST ABOUT ASSAS-SINATION.

EVEN A MASTER CHEMIST...
世界史
...TURNS INTO AN ORDINARY STUDENT BEFORE KORO SENSEI.
WE'RE STILL ...
...FAR FROM BEING THE SKILLED ASSASSINS WHO CAN KILL KORO SENSEI.
I SEE ...
BUT DON'T YOU THINK...
...THAT MIGHT FRIGHTEN THE STUDENTS?

KARA-SUMA...
WHAT'S WORSE? FRIGHTENING THE STUDENTS? OR PANICKING THE ENTIRE WORLD?
BUT...
THIS IS AN ORDER!
WE DON'T BELIEVE THOSE CHILDREN ARE CAPABLE OF KILLING HIM.
SO...
...WHAT IS THIS... OPERATIVE... LIKE?
VERY SKILLED...
ELEVEN CONFIRMED AROUND THE WORLD.

WE'RE SENDING IN...
...A REAL PROFESSIONAL.
LICK
TO BE CONTINUED...

RECESS: KORO SENSEI'S DRAWING SONG

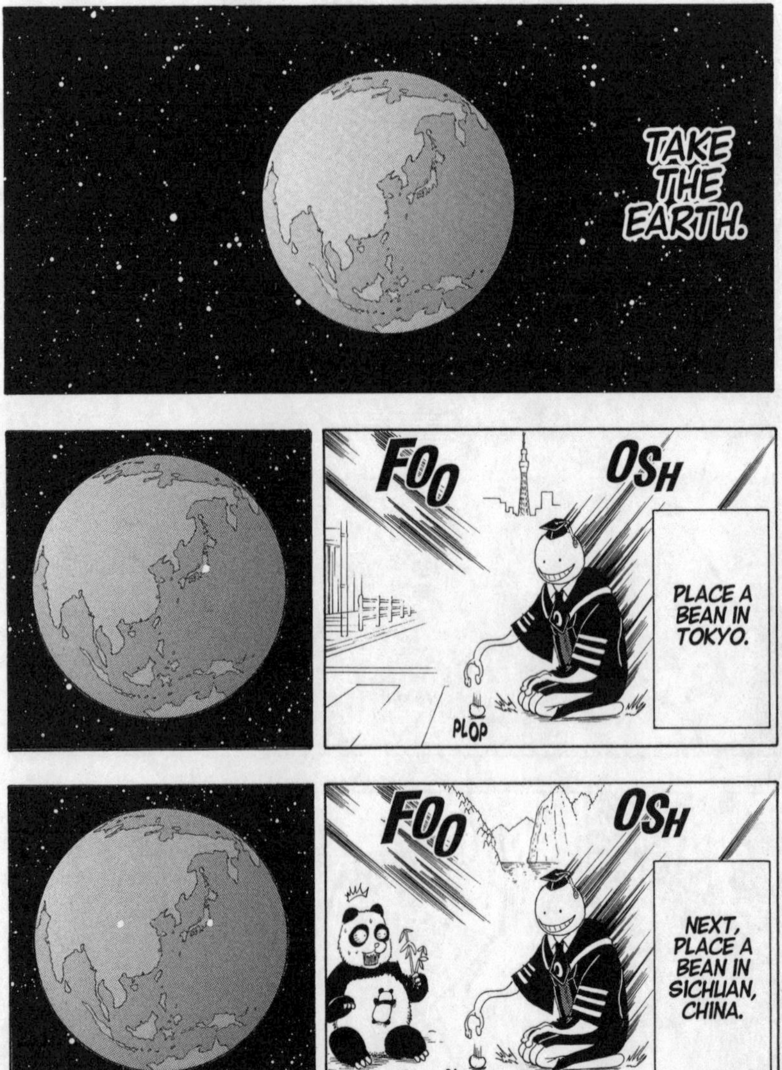
TAKE THE EARTH.
FOO OSH
PLACE A BEAN IN TOKYO.
PLOP
FOO OSH
NEXT, PLACE A BEAN IN SICHUAN, CHINA.
PLOP

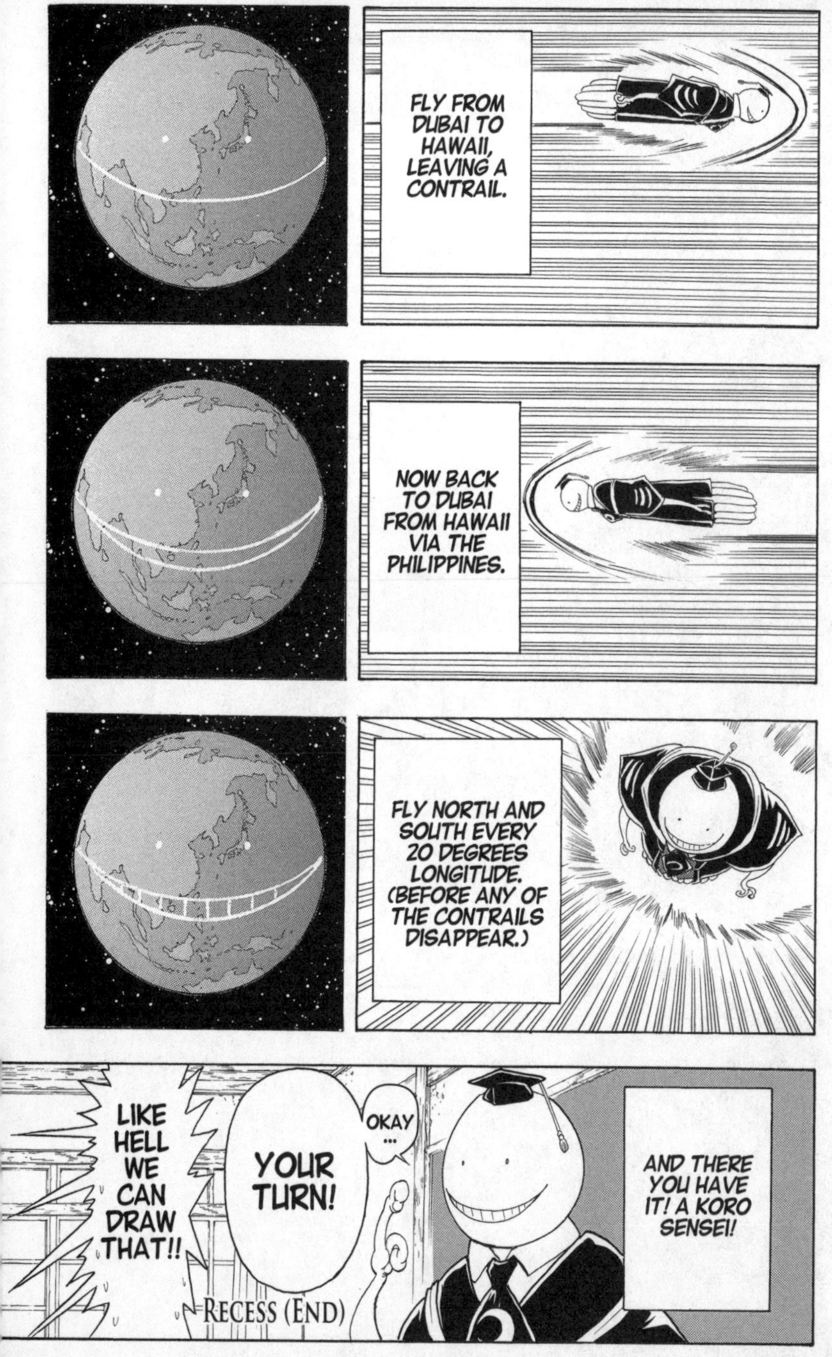
FLY FROM DUBAI TO HAWAII, LEAVING A CONTRAIL.
NOW BACK TO DUBAI FROM HAWAII VIA THE PHILIPPINES.
FLY NORTH AND SOUTH EVERY 20 DEGREES LONGITUDE. (BEFORE ANY OF THE CONTRAILS DISAPPEAR.)
AND THERE YOU HAVE IT! A KORO SENSEI!
OKAY...
YOUR TURN!
LIKE HELL WE CAN DRAW THAT!!
RECESS (END)

"Kill" is a fascinating word. It's often used, but rarely put into action.

So I decided to create a story centered around this unique word.

If you enjoy it, you can kill me now and I'll die happy.

—Yusei Matsui

Yusei Matsui was born on the last day of January in Saitama Prefecture, Japan. He has been drawing manga since elementary school. Some of his favorite manga series are *Bobobo-bo Bo-bobo*, *JoJo's Bizarre Adventure* and *Ultimate Muscle*. Matsui learned his trade working as an assistant to manga artist Yoshio Sawai, creator of *Bobobo-bo Bo-bobo*. In 2005, Matsui debuted his original manga *Neuro: Supernatural Detective* in *Weekly Shonen Jump*. In 2007, *Neuro* was adapted into an anime. In 2012, *Assassination Classroom* began serialization in *Weekly Shonen Jump*.

Yellow is his usual face color. Koro Sensei often changes the color of his face, but this is the one you'll see most often.

ASSASSINATION CLASSROOM

YUSEI MATSUI

1

TIME FOR ASSASSINATION

A MOMENT OF TENTACLE ZEN

I have no idea what kind of weapon will be used in World War III. But World War IV will be fought with tentacles.

—Koro Sensei

ASSASSINATION CLASSROOM

Volume 1
SHONEN JUMP Manga Edition

Story and Art by YUSEI MATSUI

Translation/Tetsuichiro Miyaki
English Adaptation/Bryant Turnage
Touch-up Art & Lettering/Stephen Dutro
Cover & Interior Design/Sam Elzway
Editor/Annette Roman

First published in Japan in 2012 by SHUEISHA Inc., Tokyo.
English translation rights arranged by SHUEISHA Inc.

Printed in the U.S.A.

Published by VIZ Media, LLC
P.O. Box 77010
San Francisco, CA 94107

11
First printing, December 2014
Eleventh printing, September 2020

VIZ MEDIA
viz.com

SHONEN JUMP
shonenjump.com

Syllabus for
Assassination Classroom, Vol. 2

A sexy new teacher comes to Class 3-E to do the students' job for them. When the 3-E students begin exhibiting signs of self-esteem, Principal Asano demands that Koro Sensei crush their spirits so they continue to set a bad example for the rest of the school to rise above. But Koro Sensei has other plans... Then a class field trip goes terribly wrong after two 3-E girls are abducted. Who will come to their rescue...?

Available Now!

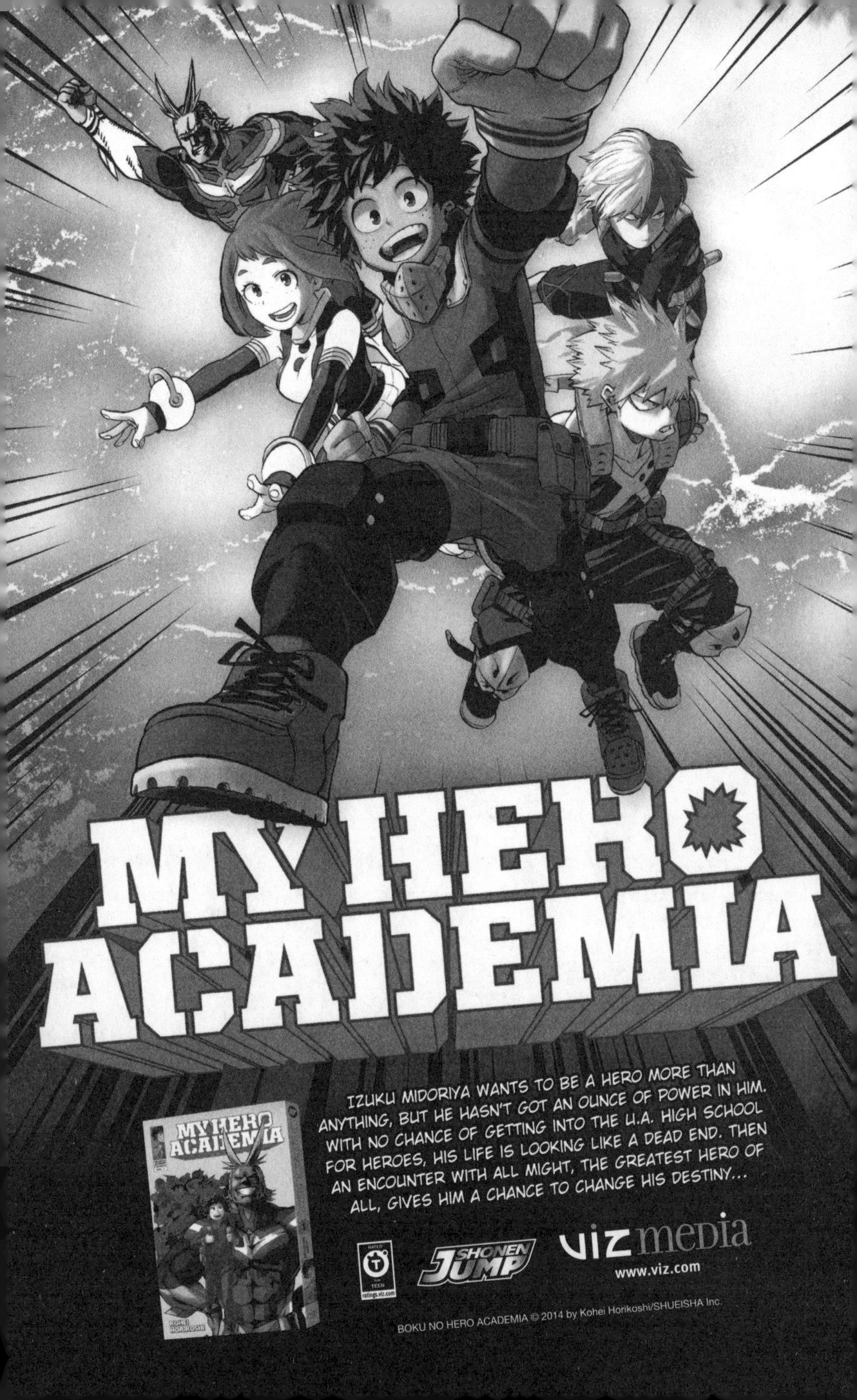
MY HERO ACADEMIA
IZUKU MIDORIYA WANTS TO BE A HERO MORE THAN ANYTHING, BUT HE HASN'T GOT AN OUNCE OF POWER IN HIM. WITH NO CHANCE OF GETTING INTO THE U.A. HIGH SCHOOL FOR HEROES, HIS LIFE IS LOOKING LIKE A DEAD END. THEN AN ENCOUNTER WITH ALL MIGHT, THE GREATEST HERO OF ALL, GIVES HIM A CHANCE TO CHANGE HIS DESTINY...
MY HERO ACADEMIA
KOHEI HORIKOSHI
RATED T TEEN
ratings.viz.com
SHONEN JUMP
VIZ media
www.viz.com
BOKU NO HERO ACADEMIA © 2014 by Kohei Horikoshi/SHUEISHA Inc.

SHOYO HINATA IS OUT TO PROVE THAT IN VOLLEYBALL YOU DON'T NEED TO BE TALL TO FLY!
HAIKYU!!
Story and Art by HARUICHI FURUDATE
Ever since he saw the legendary player known as the "Little Giant" compete at the national volleyball finals, Shoyo Hinata has been aiming to be the best volleyball player ever! He decides to join the team at the high school the Little Giant went to—and then surpass him. Who says you need to be tall to play volleyball when you can jump higher than anyone else?
viz media
www.viz.com
SHONEN JUMP
TEEN
ratings.viz.com
HAIKYU!! © 2012 by Haruichi Furudate/SHUEISHA Inc.

You're Reading in the Wrong Direction!!

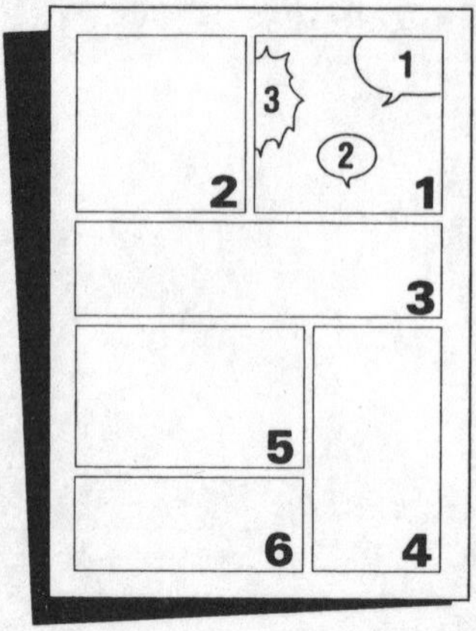

Whoops! Guess what? You're starting at the wrong end of the comic!

...It's true! In keeping with the original Japanese format, **Assassination Classroom** is meant to be read from right to left, starting in the upper-right corner.

Unlike English, which is read from left to right, Japanese is read from right to left, meaning that action, sound effects and word-balloon order are completely reversed... something which can make readers unfamiliar with Japanese feel pretty backwards themselves. For this reason, manga or Japanese comics published in the U.S. in English have sometimes been published "flopped"—that is, printed in exact reverse order, as though seen from the other side of a mirror.

By flopping pages, U.S. publishers can avoid confusing readers, but the compromise is not without its downside. For one thing, a character in a flopped manga series who once wore in the original Japanese version a T-shirt emblazoned with "M A Y" (as in "the merry month of") now wears one which reads "Y A M"! Additionally, many manga creators in Japan are themselves unhappy with the process, as some feel the mirror-imaging of their art skews their original intentions.

We are proud to bring you Yusei Matsui's **Assassination Classroom** in the original unflopped format.

For now, though, turn to the other side of the book and let the adventure begin...!

—Editor